# "NOW I SEE"

## THE STORY OF THE MAN BORN BLIND

By Marilyn Lashbrook

Illustrated by Stephanie McFetridge Britt

ME TOO! BOOKS

ROPER PRESS, INC.
DALLAS, TEXAS

The book "NOW I SEE" tells the
story of a blind man who receives
his sight and much more. Young
children often respond to handicaps
with curiosity and compassion. To
help your little one understand
blindness, turn off the lights at night
for a minute as you talk about the
man who never saw anything but
darkness. As you read the story,
pause at the designated words and
allow your child to say the word and/
or point to the picture. This story will
help your child learn about God's love
and His desire to heal our hurts. Your
little one will also learn that it is not
enough just to know about Jesus.
We must respond to Him with faith
and obedience.

Library of Congress Catalog Card Number: 88-62520
ISBN 0-86606-437-0

Art direction and design by
   Chris Schechner Graphic Design

# "NOW I SEE"

## THE STORY OF THE MAN BORN BLIND

By Marilyn Lashbrook

Illustrated by Stephanie McFetridge Britt

Taken from John 9

ME TOO!
BOOKS

Once there was a man
who had been blind
since he was born.
He had never seen anything
but darkness.

He loved the smell of warm *bread*,
but he did not know what bread looked like.

He could feel the silky fur of a *puppy*,
but he could not see a puppy.

He could hear the sweet song
of a *bird* outside his window,
but he had never seen a little bird.

Not even once.

One day, Jesus walked by.
He felt sorry for the blind man,
so He stopped to help.

Smoosh! The man felt cold, wet
mud on his eyes.
And then he heard the kindest voice
he had ever heard …
"Go to the pool and wash."

The man did not argue.
He just obeyed.

He went to the pool and washed his face.

Blink! Blink! Blink!
He opened his eyes wide.
He could see!

At last he could see blue *water*
and yellow and orange *fish*
and white *ducks* and red *flowers*

and green *frogs*
and purple *butterflies*
and anything else there was to see.

When the man came home seeing,
his neighbors wanted to know
how it happened.

The man told them that
Jesus had healed him.

But the people did not believe him.
They said terrible things about Jesus.

Then they sent the man away.

Jesus heard what the people
had said to the man.

So Jesus came to find him.

"Do you believe in
the Son of God?" Jesus asked.
The man wanted to know more.

"Tell me who He is so I can believe!"

"You are looking at Him," Jesus answered.
And the man said,
"Lord, I believe! I believe in You!"

"Listen," said the man to his neighbors,
"I have something to say.

Jesus, God's Son, healed me *twice* today!"

"My eyes were blind,
but now I *see*.

My heart was blind,
but now I *believe*."

**ME TOO!**
B O O K S

---

For Ages 2-5

**SOMEONE TO LOVE**
THE STORY OF CREATION

**"GET LOST LITTLE BROTHER"**
THE STORY OF JOSEPH

**TWO BY TWO**
THE STORY OF NOAH'S FAITH

**THE WALL THAT DID NOT FALL**
THE STORY OF RAHAB'S FAITH

**"I DON'T WANT TO"**
THE STORY OF JONAH

**NO TREE FOR CHRISTMAS**
THE STORY OF JESUS' BIRTH

**"I MAY BE LITTLE"**
THE STORY OF DAVID'S GROWTH

**"NOW I SEE"**
THE STORY OF THE MAN BORN BLIND

**"I'LL PRAY ANYWAY"**
THE STORY OF DANIEL

**DON'T ROCK THE BOAT!**
THE STORY OF THE MIRACULOUS CATCH

**WHO NEEDS A BOAT?**
THE STORY OF MOSES

**OUT ON A LIMB**
THE STORY OF ZACCHAEUS

**ME TOO!**
R E A D E R S

---

For Ages 5-8

**IT'S NOT MY FAULT**
MAN'S BIG MISTAKE

**NOTHING TO FEAR**
JESUS WALKS ON WATER

**GOD, PLEASE SEND FIRE!**
ELIJAH AND THE PROPHETS OF BAAL

**THE BEST DAY EVER**
THE STORY OF JESUS

**TOO BAD, AHAB!**
NABOTH'S VINEYARD

**THE GREAT SHAKE-UP**
MIRACLES IN PHILIPPI

**THE WEAK STRONGMAN**
SAMSON

**TWO LADS AND A DAD**
THE PRODIGAL SON

Available at your local
bookstore
or from
Roper Press
4737-A Gretna
Dallas, Texas 75207
**1-800-284-0158**